BLACK BALLAD

poems

AFUA ANSONG

DURHAM, NC

BLACK BALLAD

Library of Congress Cataloging-in-Publication Data

Names: Ansong, Afua, 1993- author.
Title: Black ballad poems / Afua Ansong.
Description: Durham, NC : Bull City Press, [2021]
Identifiers: LCCN 2021062741 | ISBN 9781949344264 (paperback)
Subjects: LCGFT: Poetry.
Classification: LCC PS3601.N555345 B53 2021 | DDC 811/.6--dc23
LC record available at https://lccn.loc.gov/2021062741

Published in the United States of America
Book design by Spock and Associates

S P O C K

Cover artwork: Paul Maen
Author photograph: Maria Baranova

Published by
BULL CITY PRESS
1217 Odyssey Drive
Durham, NC 27713
www.BullCityPress.com

CONTENTS

What Saved the Black Woman 3

I Am Not African 4

NSOROMMA 5

Postcard to Phillis Wheatley Peters 6

Petrichor 7

Home Age 8

Your First Time in America 9

Black Ballad 10

Lineage: A Conversation with a Literary Mother 11

Queen of the Early 12

Black Ballad II 13

Palm Reader 14

Counting Bodies 16

Good Friday 17

HYE WONHYE 18

Cocoa 19

Reincarnation 20

Unidentified 21

Elegy 22

The Undoing 23

Rebellion 24

Foreign City 25

Things You Left in Accra before Moving to the Bronx 26

ODO NNYEW FIE KWAN 27

sɛ wo werɛ fi na wo sankofa a yɛnkyi

Don't worry, it is not taboo to return to what was once forgotten.

—Akan Proverb

WHAT SAVED THE BLACK WOMAN

I am born twice: first in retrospect and second
into the arms of defiance. Mother's blood soils
a dirty Accra hospital. I don't delay in her womb,
drinking her strength. Father returns from London
and stays. He watches me grow into a full tree
of Kwahu girl. Pimples the size of meteors
don't etch holes in my face. Smoke from the rain
cools the air. Mother returns from London with a black
suitcase full of pounds. Mother stays. *I beg you mother*
to stay. Don't complicate this myth of a woman leaving
to bring her children gold. I don't discover that pickling
trouble is like exchanging sweet for salt. We delight
in the dust of Accra. I burn from the seeds
of my grandmother's wild peppers. Father still loses his job.
Mother sells bottles and I sell my body to a Minister
with piles of citizens' papers on his desk. I am not ashamed
because it pays for tuition and a trip to the market. I believe
in something but it is not God. It is shaped like the curves
of my ears and tastes like rust. Poetry does not save me,
but how can this be? But how can this be?

I AM NOT AFRICAN

We need new names.

I am that Odum wood
the carpenter saws for his mother's
coffin. See that jacaranda popping

petals of grace and lavender?

I am that brown branch
bending the back of a butterfly
asking, asking

if the skies have shaken hands

for rain to fall and faith to sprout.
No, not even "West African Sepia."
I am not African. I have only known

the red sands behind my grandmother's garden,
the silver dove sitting under the moon.

NSOROMMA
children of heaven

To say something is unexpected is to suggest
that it is a surprise, usually unpleasant: you wonder about the damage
it could have caused. Your mother reminds you that you were unexpected
but wanted, like the tree of knowledge of good & evil to test man's disobedience.

She was not surprised: your mother accused your father of bringing her some disease
& she had grown lean with you inside her & we don't know how frightened Eve
was when she perceived a serpent could talk, or how alarmed your mother was
that you would lie in her belly for ten months & drink no breast milk after you left
the sac of a womb.

So Eve communed with the serpent & man minded his own business
& your father hoped no disease had carried him & you finally slept
in someone's arm, unexpected.

The crunch of the fruit on her jaw as Eve bit into disobedience, unexpected,
your mother sucking on the seed of conception three years after having her previous child,
shocked because it was supposed to be four & some garden breeze whistling history
into present & Eve not surprised that this was expected to her maker.

POSTCARD TO PHILLIS WHEATLEY PETERS

They say they cannot find you, where you are
from, Senegambia or so, a land where women eat
gold to heal their skins and soften their gums.

They could not erase your voice. You wrote
to surprise yourself; possessed by the spirit
of language. You disentombed the stories
lined in the cartilage of your eardrums.
Your mothers must have sat by rivers to listen
to the way fish wept when currents flowed.

Strangeness followed you like a bee in labor.
Some white men sat you in a room and asked
if you wrote poetry; that a Black woman could place
neat rhymes shocked their sensibilities.
Yes is all you must have said to keep gratitude
in your teeth, anger in your wrist.

I want to say *thank you*. I am a woman
who is often not given a room to light
fires and burn bias. I accept the layers
of this skin. I desire myself as I would
a bag of hot rocks near my feet in winter.

Whoever you really are because you are
somebody, descendant of queens, griotess
—that is what we shall call you! I can feel it
when the finger I left in my mother's womb quivers.

PETRICHOR

You ask Imani, which means *faith*,
to bring back sand from the continent

you have avoided for years—
you yearn to inhale part of that world.

Perhaps you should have asked for
a cup of wind and dust from Accra

with the scent of mud, and melodies
from mating wasps, but South

Africa was her destination.

She returns with rocks
that smell of cold sunrises

but nothing like the heat from Tema
explodes from the sand when you

pour it into a vase
you've labeled *home*.

You quarantine yourself in this black
body and dream an escape to Cape Coast

where you know what settles
beneath the erupting earth.

HOME AGE

I am of the spilling pockets of loquacious market women from Kwahu,
Women who lick the front side of a cedi with the faces of Black men
who passed batons of independence until honor required their deaths,

Women who know the taste of money weakens & begging is insufficient,
Women who balance sand on their heads and keep arms akimbo for style:

Women who say the same mouth used for begging can never be the same that shames,
Women who say food will be ready soon but have now planted the seeds,

Women who know how to lie when their breasts are in a man's mouth,
Women who know how to take money from their men when their lips
are in a man's ear, Women who beat their children with their mouths,

Women who laugh when they die before their children, Women who cry
to their mothers when their men bring a child from another woman,
Women who clean their bodies with oils and comb their hair with iron.

YOUR FIRST TIME IN AMERICA

You arrive in a darkness that blunts the city's fangs
because America hides its ugly with lights.

The drive is slow like the tires want you to see
that with all the gleaming eyes at the airport,

you almost missed your mother adorned in a lavender
blouse with matching slippers. She emerged as though

she had come to greet her lover and not the daughters
who slipped from her hands for six years. Absence

is the cousin of darkness. Accra is full of darkness too,
no charms, just a few unwanted prayer altars

built over spilled blood and nagging gods.
You reach the Bronx and your mother offers you her bed.

She sleeps on the floor. The noise of the city is a blanket of light.
In the morning, 169th Street reminds you of your grandmother's

dirty village park. In your apartment, roaches float on wooden wings,
rodents burrow holes with rotten teeth and hungry bellies.

You are bitter when your tight brown curls reveal
the way you look just like your mother without her gap tooth.

BLACK BALLAD

Black boy don't you dare! But he smiles and his teeth pull you in. Night. You are both in the back seat now. You reach Canton at 12:01 a.m., just as the train promised. Your mother's voice eats into your ears, but you refuse to call her and recite words like *I'm safe* even though all the trees branch in awkward bends and raise your pressure. The darkness tightens your legs and your suitcases don't breathe. You notice a police car driving back and forth like a noxious predator. The smell of Christmas, which is just cold air and pines, lines your nostrils. The man with dreadlocks follows you. You are riding with a Black man next to you in a police car. You tell him you are lost. He opens the back seat of the police car and you look away. He tells you a woman's instinct is often right. The news tells you not to trust the liquid sirens. And he is alive. You see him enter and your guts shrink. Black woman, you are alive too.

LINEAGE: A CONVERSATION WITH A LITERARY MOTHER

—so I called Lucille
to tell me stories
of her mother
and she said
child, to be a poet
is to hurt
like the ribs of Eve.
Everyday
your blood
must taste
the blood of men:
savage, black, worn.
You must dare to bite
into things that call
for exile, call for God's
anger and send down
a savior.

QUEEN OF THE EARLY

I grew a child once
from warm clay: her perfume,
roasted tropical almonds.

I watched her as a seed
washed her feet,
as they sprouted to peek
at the moon
and waited ninety days
for her head to ripen.

When her skin cracked
to unveil her flesh,
I cut off her vibrant flowers,
plucked her womb.

A worthy prize for market:
fresh, organic, virgin.

BLACK BALLAD II

We did not eat snails that day.
Not after we heard N'akuma was dead.
I asked my grandmother if she was
the same woman that sat on our dark
blue couch. She'd always wear a silk head-wrap
and when I'd eavesdrop on their talks,
I would hear the names of brothers, uncles, & aunties
whose bodies were now caged in coffins. A week before,
she'd brought us a pan of thin fried fish covered
with white lace. As if when she walked through
the crowded market, no one dared to touch her.
Who knew that giving fish as gift meant moving
on to the next life? My grandmother,
she cried, mourned, rocked herself to comfort.
Grandma gyae su, but she would not hear me.
In her wails, she asked her cousin
Have you seen it,
What we spoke about—do you know when it will come for me?

PALM READER

From my room, I hear my mother say
breast cancer and sing a low *oww*.

She repeats what her aunt says,
lemon leaves mixed with something sweet.

When she hangs up the phone,
she whispers, *she must have been in pain*
recovering from these scars alone.

My breasts are small, young mountains
in my cupped hands. The left line in both
palms leans further in from the right.

I want to grow lemon trees to erase diseases
from my bloodline. The spaces between my fingers

are islands. I lay my body there to rest.
The stub to my eleventh finger breathes

a genuine rhetoric. If one member is removed,
a string of memories remains. The mother
to my mother's mother wore life for seventy years.

The folds in my palm bend my hands to age.
The taste of lineage is sour, sour, running rancid.

COUNTING BODIES

At the   Bx19 bus stop

      Black boys   to my right

count bodies—   fog on the lips of Spring—

      one boasts   of sixteen   and the other   short

with a backpack   hugging his thin

      back says   seventeen.   He hits   the timid one

in the stomach, who yells,   *I'm not a virgin.*

      They leave him alone.   They must be fifteen and a half.

I stare   at fat pigeons folded   on telephone poles

and count   all six of them.   I chant,   *stay alive, stay alive, stay alive.*

GOOD FRIDAY

Mama says I'm killing Jesus
again every time I return home
        and hand her a check from another
man. She sees my skin oily
from his sweat. In my dreams,
        the three-footed serpent tells me
my body belongs to him and
I hear lamentations
        from my dead father's wisdom tooth,
still soiled from an uproot.
We don't need the money anymore she says.
        He's dead and my tomatoes are selling well.
But how do I retrace my steps
to the tomb for resurrection?
        How do I return my body to myself?

HYE WONHYE
burn, but you won't burn

In burning the female butterflies,
the boys sing until the clouds close.

They clap and stamp in unison
as monarchs with green and yellow

ovals printed on their wings hit the coal.
Their legs shake and they raise

antennas into the smoke.
The scent of the burning stings like palm

wine melting in the throat of a tree.
Hye wonhye, their chants rise.

The eagle that maps the view of the sky,
vast and lush, knows the boys inhale a flame

that morphs them into kings.

COCOA

Maame brings it to us,
says she knows the cocoa, what it tastes like,
as if she met Fernão do Pó, who held her hands
as they ripped the fruits from trees in the dry forest.

We wait, watch her slam the pod on the ground.
ten-year-old girls with no knives between our thighs,
we wonder why

it is yellow & not black. She tells us to pluck with our teeth
& suck the white seeds with saliva, tells us *you are eating cocoa,*
tangy & welcoming. I hold the buttons of my uniform
to feel the smoothness of my chest instead, though Esi's is ripe.
My season brings me nothing.

I ask Maame, *what should we do after we swallow the sap?*
& she says to spit it out.

REINCARNATION

&

yes,

I died a black swan and

woke,

sharp, in the skin of

Mitochondrial Eve.

A

shadow falls

on me like

a cold look and

suddenly my hairs rise, pupils

dilate, and this almond-shaped amygdala

shivers. A continuous reverberation of light wings

flaps at my face. This is absurd, for on my wall, right down that

American hall, hangs a painting; a mythical conga bird

perched on a tree branch. Next to this, a picture of mother

& me in Accra. I wake

to beads of sweat lining my back and

copper collarbone.

On my wrist I latch, each day,

a crystal hummingbird. It

plucks nectar from fuchsia petals

as it ticks and talks the time of

my world, where my niece's curled

upper lip and my cousin's small

nose are mirrors

of my grandmother's golden

face.

UNIDENTIFIED

[of the 200 plus Adinkra symbols I surveyed at the Fowler Museum, a few were labeled *unidentified*]

When my eyes close, there is a well.
When I open my mouth for air,
you are here too, don't you know?

Your insistence, the tapping of your small feet.
You tell me to think of something clean: the Sunday afternoon
I avoided a snake that almost bit me or the day it rained so hard
after the sun melted grandma's pepper leaves.
The ants wished they could fly in the cold Accra rain.

ELEGY

The night before you kill yourself, you pluck seeds from the moon with your teeth
to see the wound of a boy who gets shot in the shoulders at a gas
station next to your apartment. The demons take note.

You lie on the rubber covering your bed and lock your accent under your tongue,
against your ancestor's lament. You remember an encounter with a lame woman
who told you loons could walk over the lake and how she'd hope God
would make her feet wide.

No deliverance exists tonight for you or the boy, but you feel as American as ever.
You will both sleep until Resurrection's dawn or maybe the spirit that wants you gone
will yoke with the dark clouds and present you to an afterlife.

Your mothers will clean the mess. Your burials will be neat.
You will be loans to your nation, long gone, and only a name.

THE UNDOING

The same breaking

The same uproot

The same breath

The same ripping

The same stitches

The same knife

The same teeth

The same leaving

The same surrender

The same bullet

The same resurrecting

Out of flesh

Out of rhythm

Out of green

Out of stone

Out of its emptying cage

REBELLION

after Lucille Clifton

Won't you celebrate her:
left her country at fourteen,
lost her identity at sixteen,
discovered she couldn't return at eighteen,
contemplated suicide at twenty and twenty-one
and on certain occasions, like
last Tuesday, she found herself
at the knees of poetry
and every word that has tried
to kill her grows as a new layer
of black skin.

FOREIGN CITY

In the Bronx or Accra, whatever you now call it—
because the texture of language reminds you, you are not home—
you think a lot about what the surprise of morning
over the gossiping mango trees felt like in that city, not this city.
Of the city, not that city but this, how pounding the flesh
of boiled palm nuts soils the mortar,
first red then yellow. You thank the fruit of life,
in your inner chambers where fire grows from your hands.

THINGS YOU LEFT IN ACCRA BEFORE MOVING TO THE BRONX

Grandma and her weak leg,
your sister at eighteen, still with one good iris,

your mother's British jewelry hidden under the bed,
the places in the carpet you soiled with urine,

all the red dust,

your seat at Calvary Methodist Church next to Marie
who'd always chat with you when someone talked
about Jesus & his power to bring you all the things you needed,

your gymnastic booty shorts (your mother sent
them from America because the heat in Accra overwhelmed
you but you still wish you'd saved some for America's winters),

warm Tea Bread sold at the YMCA between 6:30 & 7:30 a.m.,
the scent of air conditioning & ice cream at the Shell gas station,

Grandma with her good English,

Mercedes & Pamela, your neighbors who borrowed everything from salt to ladles,

Asaana, Yooyi, Aluguntuguin, Nkontomire,
Living Bitters, Mercy Cream, Lion's Ointment &

a Saturday listening to wind turn on pawpaw leaves.

ODO NNYEW FIE KWAN
love never loses its way home

The white pulp of the cocoa seeds, heaven's fruit,
swells on my tongue. In Accra, rain soaks into the rigid throat
of Harmattan & floods my spongy black coils.
Angels wish they had lips to suck an answer out of God's mouth.

Weeds on a beans farm. Mother's placenta
shrunken after childbirth. The long hands that broke
this pod empty & sweat around my face. The cocoa still
in the feet of the soil. Mother not yet eaten
by a red beast called Woman. Father sleeping
under a cave & eating termites for dinner.
He calls it home but chews small stones instead of bones.

I buckle up as the plane grates its wheels
on Ghana's soil. I am glad I am not on a ship.
I pray I'll never be in chains. My plump thighs itch
with each turbulence. Accra's red moonlight drowns my wails.

The shapes of letters remain in my jaws
for a name like mine. The claws of these yellow teeth
biting at my girlhood without a mother. America.
Even when she sent for me, I left
my knees at Aburi gardens.
I walk the continent raging in tongues.

Inside, my sister shatters mother's full-length mirror
with a punch. Outside, I place my pinkie in a socket
& currents rock my two-year-old house. Inside,

I dance backward & crack my skull & blood gathers.
Outside, a bat waits for night. Inside, Hope
is our brown dog with a wagging tail. Outside, Hope
is hit by a car & the driver has a wagging finger.

The Bronx clouds like cocoa pods break
over my sweet black body. Angels fall:
they teach me ways to catch myself.

I am grateful to these journals where earlier versions of these poems first appeared:

"Postcard to Phillis Wheatley Peters" – *Cincinnati Review*
"Things You Left in Accra before Moving to the Bronx" – *Florida Review*
"Queen of the Early" – *FOLIO*
"Black Ballad" – *Four Way Review*
"Palm Reader" – *Prairie Schooner*
"I Am Not African" – *Seventh Wave*
"Good Friday" – *Vinyl Poetry*

"What Saved the Black Woman" first appeared as "Born Again" in the chapbook *American Mercy*, published by Finishing Line Press.

I am grateful to the Water Mill Center in Long Island, where much of this work was heavily revised, and to my advisor Peter Covino, who supported this work immensely. Thank you Levis Keltner for seeing potential in earlier drafts of this collection.

This book is for my mother, who sings her poems and stories through me.

ABOUT THE AUTHOR

AFUA ANSONG is a scholar and artist currently completing a Ph.D. in English Literature at the University of Rhode Island. She is an advocate of Black/ African women's voices. Her work interrogates representations of Black female subjectivities in African Diaspora Literature. She is working on a collection of poems about the material culture and poetic elements of the Adinkra symbols from Ghana. Specifically, she is recording how West African oral art serves as a mode of expression and survival for enslaved Akans in bondage. She has two chapbooks, *Try Kissing God* (Akashic, 2020) and *American Mercy* (Finishing Line Press, 2019), and has published work in *Prairie Schooner, Four Way Review, Maine Review,* and other journals. She has received scholarships from Bread Loaf and Blue Mountain Center. More of her work is at *afuansong.com.*

This book was published with assistance from the Fall 2020 Editing and Publishing class at the University of North Carolina at Chapel Hill. Contributing editors and designers were Madeline Chandler, Eli Hardwig, Mia Powell, and Jordan Snow.